Very Merry Cocktails

50+

Festive Drinks *for the* Holiday Season

Very Merry Cocktails

JESSICA STRAND

Photographs by **REN FULLER**

CHRONICLE BOOKS

SAN FRANCISCO

Library of Congress Cataloging-in-Publication Data

Names: Strand, Jessica, author. | Fuller, Ren, photographer.
Title: Very merry cocktails / Jessica Strand ; photographs by Ren Fuller.
Description: San Francisco : Chronicle Books, [2020] | Includes index.
Identifiers: LCCN 2019054985 | ISBN 9781452184708 (hardcover) | ISBN 9781797200385 (ebook)
Subjects: LCSH: Cocktails. | Beverages.
Classification: LCC TX951 .S895 2020 | DDC 641.87/4--dc23
LC record available at https://lccn.loc.gov/2019054985

Manufactured in China.

MIX
Paper from responsible sources
FSC
www.fsc.org   FSC™ C008047

Design by Lizzie Vaughan.
Recipe development and testing by Dena Rayess.
Prop styling by Stephanie Hanes.
Food styling by Marian Cooper Cairns.
Assistant food styling by Michelle Ferrand.
Typeset in Avenir Next, Canopee, and Fazeta.

Angostura is a registered trademark of Angostura International Limited Company; Bailey's is a registered trademark of R & A Bailey & Co; Bombay Sapphire Gin is a registered trademark of Bacardi & Company Limited; Bundt is a registered trademark of Northland Aluminum Products, Inc.; Campari is a registered trademark of Davide Campari - Milano S.P.A.; Chambord is a registered trademark of Brown-Forman Corporation; Clamato is a registered trademark of Mott's LLP; Cointreau is a registered trademark of Cointreau Corp.; Fireball is a registered trademark of Sazerac Brands, LLC; Grand Marnier is a registered trademark of Marnier-Lapostolle Bisquit SA; Kahlúa is a registered trademark of The Absolut Company Aktiebolag; La Croix is a registered trademark of Everfresh Beverages, Inc.; Lillet is a registered trademark of Societe Lillet Freres; Pimm's is a registered trademark of Diageo Brands B.V.; Sofia is a registered trademark of GMYL, L.P. Sentinel Corp.; St-Germain is a registered trademark of Bacardi & Company Limited; Tabasco is a registered trademark of McIlhenny Company; Worcestershire is a registered trademark of H.J. Heinz US Brands LLC.

10 9 8 7 6 5 4 3 2 1

Chronicle books and gifts are available at special quantity discounts to corporations, professional associations, literacy programs, and other organizations. For details and discount information, please contact our premiums department at corporatesales@chroniclebooks.com or at 1-800-759-0190.

Chronicle Books LLC
680 Second Street
San Francisco, CA 94107
www.chroniclebooks.com

FA

LA LA

LA LA LA

CONTENTS

CHAPTER 1
'TIS THE SEASON COCKTAILS 28

CHAPTER 2
FESTIVE CHAMPAGNE SIPPERS 64

INTRODUCTION

I love when the weather cools down, the days grow shorter, and our family gears up for the holiday season. We hang a wreath on the door, trim a tree with yards of flickering lights, and tack mistletoe to the most-traveled doorway in our home. With this seasonal decorating comes the fun of planning holiday parties: My husband and I pull out our favorite seasonal tunes, stoke the fire, and open our doors to friends and family for hearty food and festive drinks.

That's where this book comes in. Here, you'll find more than fifty recipes for classic holiday drinks, as well as clever new concoctions that may quickly become favorites. I hope that among them, you'll find holiday cheer and perhaps even inspiration for a party theme. Let your libations set the tone for a sophisticated craft cocktail party, a homey post-shopping get-together, or a romantic tête-à-tête on a snowy night.

All the recipes in this book emphasize the celebratory nature of the holiday season with strong flavors, seasonal garnishes, and striking colors. 'Tis the Season Cocktails are fun, festive drinks, made to order. Perhaps you'd like a Mistletoe Kiss (page 50), a tart, sweet tequila concoction finished with a drop of bright grenadine? Or try the Fireside Glow (page 54), a booze-forward riff on a Fireball—perfect for warming up on cold nights. Festive Champagne Sippers suit the most glamorous occasions. Consider a ruby-toned Kir Royale (page 79) for a romantic aperitif on Christmas Eve, or a tray of Holiday Bellinis (page 72) to ring in the New Year. Warm & Toasty Toddies, on the other hand, lend a comforting, homespun touch. Hot Mint Chocolate (page 84), made with peppermint schnapps, is welcomed après-ski or while caroling on a cold winter's night. Perfect for a crowd, Holiday Party Punches are simple to make and encourage mingling around the punch bowl. This section offers a range of choices, from Classic Eggnog (page 106) to spicy Wassail (page 108). For nondrinkers and kids, Zero-Proof Libations ensure they don't feel left out of the party. Offer them a quenching Gingersnap Punch (page 114), made with ginger ale, raspberry syrup, and lime juice, or a rich Foamy Mexican Hot Chocolate (page 122) with a dollop of fresh Whipped Cream (page 25). No matter the occasion, there is something here for everyone.

So mix a cocktail for yourself and a friend, and toast to the season and all the joy it brings. Cheers! Happy holidays to one and all!

BAR EQUIPMENT

Here's a simple list of bar tools that are particularly useful for making these holiday cocktails and other drinks.

BAR SPOON

This long-handled spoon is ideal for stirring drinks in a mixing glass, serving glass, or pitcher.

BAR STRAINER

This coil-rimmed strainer is necessary for straining ice out of a mixing glass or shaker.

BAR TOWEL

Not only a practical accessory for wiping up spills, decorative bar towels can also help you bring the holiday theme into any party.

CITRUS REAMER/ SQUEEZER

When you're entertaining, you don't want friends to line up for a drink while you struggle to get the last bits of juice out of your citrus. These tools speed up the job.

COCKTAIL SHAKER/ MIXING GLASS

This is an essential two-part item for shaking cocktails. The mixing glass serves as your container for stirred, not shaken, cocktails.

CORKSCREW

A basic item for any bar. Though a corkscrew is typically not needed for mixing cocktails, be sure to have one on hand for recipes that require wine, like Glögg (page 101).

ICE BUCKET & TONGS

A bucket can be both a decorative and useful item to store your ice during a party so it won't melt. It can be nice to have an extra pair of tongs set out so two guests can fill their glasses at the same time.

ICE TRAYS

Recipes in this book call for various types of ice: cubed, spherical, crushed. It may be worth investing in ice trays of different shapes and sizes—it's an easy way to dress up a drink and wow your guests!

ICE PICK/MALLET

It's helpful to have something on hand to break up the ice, but it's certainly not essential if you are using ice cubes.

JIGGER MEASURE/ SHOT GLASS

This is an extremely handy item to have around, particularly for less experienced mixologists. Look for one that has ½ oz [15 ml] gradations to help you measure accurately.

PICKS

Wooden, plastic, metal, or bamboo skewers can add a delightful touch to all kinds of garnishes. Have a variety on hand to complement the different styles of glassware in your collection.

VEGETABLE PEELER

Use this indispensable tool to create a twist of lemon, lime, or any other fruit with a hard skin.

ZESTER/STRIPPER

This is a very helpful tool that strips the rind from fruits for garnishes.

STOCKING THE HOLIDAY BAR

Because you'll be entertaining more, you'll want to stock up your bar for the holidays. The following lists include items you'll need for mixing drinks at this festive time of year. Personalize your bar by noting the kinds of drinks you and your guests prefer and choosing some fun seasonal garnishes—browse through the recipes in this book for ideas! Buy enough supplies so that you'll be prepared for drop-in visitors and last-minute get-togethers.

 ## HOLIDAY MIXERS & INGREDIENTS

Following you'll find two lists—Essentials and Extras—to help you prepare for the holiday rush. The Essentials give you the basics you need to make a wide variety of cocktails, while the Extras prepare you to whip up any of the recipes in this book.

ESSENTIALS

◊ Angostura bitters

◊ **CITRUS:** grapefruit, lemons, limes, and oranges, for juicing

◊ Clamato

◊ Club soda or seltzer

◊ Cocoa

◊ Coffee

◊ Crème de cassis

◊ **FRUIT JUICES:** apple cider, apricot nectar, cranberry, lemonade, orange, and pineapple

◊ Ginger ale

◊ Ginger beer

◊ Grenadine

◊ Heavy whipping cream, half-and-half, and whole milk

◊ **ICE:** crushed, spherical, cubes, a single large cube

◊ **SUGAR:** brown, dark brown, confectioners', and superfine

◊ Vanilla extract

EXTRAS

- ◊ Almonds, whole and blanched
- ◊ Apple cider vinegar
- ◊ Black pepper, freshly ground
- ◊ Black tea
- ◊ Butter
- ◊ Cardamom pods
- ◊ Celery stalks
- ◊ Cheese
- ◊ Creamed horseradish
- ◊ Crème de coconut
- ◊ Dill pickles
- ◊ Eggs
- ◊ Figs and fig jam
- ◊ **FRUIT JUICES:** blueberry, pomegranate, and white cranberry
- ◊ Lemonade, sparkling and still
- ◊ Malted milk powder
- ◊ Maple syrup
- ◊ Mexican hot chocolate
- ◊ Pearl onions
- ◊ Pepperoncini
- ◊ Quince paste
- ◊ Salt
- ◊ Sparkling apple cider
- ◊ Sparkling lemon water (La Croix or similar)
- ◊ Stuffed olives
- ◊ Sugar cubes
- ◊ Tabasco
- ◊ Worcestershire sauce

HOLIDAY LIQUORS

There are many brands of liquor, and you will typically find the more you spend, the smoother and better the taste. That's not to say that a less expensive alcohol will ruin a drink—do your own taste tests to decide for yourself. Consider purchasing larger bottles to get a better deal on a tastier brand. And don't worry about spoilage, since bottled spirits have an infinite shelf life.

ESSENTIALS

- ◊ Brandy
- ◊ Champagne
- ◊ **CREAM LIQUEURS:** Irish cream, such as Baileys; coffee liqueur, such as Kahlúa
- ◊ Gin
- ◊ Orange liqueur, such as Cointreau or Triple Sec
- ◊ Red wine
- ◊ Rum, both light and dark
- ◊ **SCHNAPPS:** butterscotch, peppermint, and sour apple
- ◊ Tequila
- ◊ Vermouth, both sweet and dry
- ◊ Vodka

EXTRAS

◊ Advocaat

◊ Aquavit

◊ Bombay Sapphire gin

◊ Calvados

◊ Campari

◊ Cognac

◊ **CORDIALS:** crème de cacao, amaretto, crème de menthe, Chambord, Grand Marnier, ouzo

◊ Currant vodka

◊ Elderflower liqueur

◊ Irish whiskey

◊ Lambic beer

◊ Lillet

◊ Muscat dessert wine

◊ Peach liqueur

◊ Pear eau de vie

◊ Pimm's

 # HOLIDAY GARNISHES

From lemon twists to mini candy canes and cinnamon sticks, garnishes create the mood of a drink. Most of these take just seconds to prepare, while others are more elaborate. They all add holiday flavor and festivity. Here is a list to get you thinking—and remember that some garnishes can alter the flavor of the drink, so be sure to test your own creations before serving them to a crowd.

FLAVORED RIMS

◊ Candied Citrus Slices (page 24)

◊ Cinnamon Rim (page 26)

◊ Sugar Rim (page 26)

◊ Sweet & Spicy Sugar Rim (page 26)

SWEET & SAVORY ADDITIONS

◊ Candied ginger

◊ Cinnamon sticks

◊ **CITRUS WEDGES:** lemon, lime, orange, and tangerine

◊ Cocoa

◊ Cucumbers

◊ **EDIBLE HERBS & FLOWERS:** lemon balm, rose petals, rosemary, tarragon, basil, mint, lavender, marigolds, nasturtiums, begonias, and violets

◊ Frozen blueberries

◊ Gold leaf

◊ Grapes

◊ Maraschino cherries

◊ Mini candy canes

◊ Nutmeg

◊ Olives

◊ Pears

◊ Pomegranate seeds

◊ Sliced almonds

SYRUP, SHRUB & GARNISH RECIPES

SIMPLE SYRUP

1 cup [200 g] sugar

8 oz [240 ml] water

This recipe is incredibly versatile, so feel free to explore lots of different flavors.

Combine the sugar and water in a medium saucepan over medium-high heat. Bring the mixture to a rapid boil, stirring to dissolve the sugar. Remove from the heat and let cool. Store the syrup in an airtight container in the refrigerator for up to 1 week. Makes 12 oz [355 ml].

ROSEMARY SYRUP

1 cup [200 g] sugar

8 oz [240 ml] water

3 rosemary sprigs

Combine the sugar, water, and rosemary sprigs in a medium saucepan over medium-high heat. Bring the mixture to a rapid boil, stirring to dissolve the sugar. Remove from the heat and let cool. Strain the syrup and store in an airtight container in the refrigerator for up to 1 week. Makes 12 oz [355 ml].

CINNAMON SYRUP

1 cup [200 g] sugar

8 oz [240 ml] water

1 cinnamon stick

Combine the sugar, water, and cinnamon stick in a medium saucepan over medium-high heat. Bring the mixture to a rapid boil, stirring to dissolve the sugar. Remove from the heat and let cool. Strain the syrup and store in an airtight container in the refrigerator for up to 1 week. Makes 12 oz [355 ml].

HONEY SYRUP

1 cup [340 g] mild honey, such as wildflower or orange blossom

8 oz [240 ml] water

Combine the honey and water in a medium saucepan over medium-high heat. Bring the mixture to a rapid boil, stirring occasionally. Remove from the heat and let cool. Strain the syrup and store in an airtight container in the refrigerator for up to 1 week. Makes 12 oz [355 ml].

RASPBERRY SYRUP

1 cup [200 g] sugar

8 oz [240 ml] water

1 cup [120 g] raspberries

Combine the sugar, water, and raspberries in a medium saucepan over medium-high heat. Bring the mixture to a rapid boil, stirring to dissolve the sugar. Remove from the heat and let cool. Strain the syrup and store in an airtight container in the refrigerator for up to 1 week. Makes 12 oz [355 ml].

CANDIED CITRUS SLICES & CITRUS SYRUP

1 cup [200 g] sugar

4 oz [120 ml] water

2 lemons, 2 limes, 1 orange, or 1 grapefruit, cut into ⅛ in [4 mm] slices or rounds

This recipe provides two ingredients at once. While you're candying your citrus fruit, you'll also be making a delightful citrus syrup. Feel free to candy any type of citrus fruit, including tangerines, lemons, limes, grapefruit, oranges, or kumquats.

Combine the sugar and water in a saucepan and bring to a boil. Add the citrus slices to the pan. Let the boiling syrup reduce for 5 minutes or until it begins to thicken, turning the citrus occasionally. Pull the citrus slices out and place on a piece of wax paper to cool. Cool the citrus syrup on the stove. Store the cooled slices and the syrup separately, covered, in the refrigerator. Citrus slices will keep for 2 to 3 days in the refrigerator. The citrus syrup will keep almost indefinitely. Makes 12 oz [355 ml].

CRANBERRY SHRUB

8 oz [240 ml] apple cider vinegar

1 cup [200 g] sugar

1 cup [120 g] cranberries

Heat the apple cider vinegar and sugar in a small saucepan over medium heat. Stir the mixture until the sugar fully dissolves. Add the cranberries and bring to a simmer, mashing the cranberries into the mixture as they soften. Simmer for 2 minutes and then remove from the heat. Let cool. Strain the shrub into an airtight glass container. The shrub can be stored in the refrigerator for up to 5 days. Makes 12 oz [355 ml].

WHIPPED CREAM

8 oz [240 ml] heavy
(whipping) cream

1 tsp confectioners' sugar
(optional)

Pour the cream into a large bowl.
If you want it sweetened, add the
sugar. Whip with an electric or
hand mixer until it forms stiff peaks
(be sure not to overwhip). Use
immediately. Makes 12 oz [355 ml].

BLUEBERRY-LEMON-
ROSEMARY ICE RING

1 cup [140 g] fresh blueberries

1 lemon, thinly sliced

4 rosemary sprigs

Place the blueberries, lemon slices,
and rosemary sprigs evenly around
a Bundt pan. Slowly pour in 16 to
24 oz [480 to 720 ml] water, leaving
1 to 2 in [2.5 to 5 cm] of space at
the top of the pan. Freeze until set,
4 to 5 hours or overnight. Store until
ready to serve with punch. Makes
12 oz [355 ml].

GRAPEFRUIT SHRUB

8 oz [240 ml] apple cider
vinegar

1 cup [200 g] sugar

1 grapefruit, peeled and diced

Heat the apple cider vinegar and
sugar in a small saucepan over
medium heat. Stir the mixture until
the sugar fully dissolves. Add the
grapefruit and bring to a simmer,
mashing the grapefruit into the
mixture to release as much juice as
possible. Simmer for 2 minutes and
then remove the pan from the heat.
Let cool. Strain the shrub into an
airtight glass container. The shrub
can be stored in the refrigerator for
up to 5 days. Makes 10 oz [300 ml].

HOW TO RIM A GLASS

Choose your glass. (If you want a frosted glass combined with a decorative rim, chill the glass first in the freezer for about an hour.) On a small plate wider than the rim of the glass, pour a shallow layer of superfine sugar, cocoa, cinnamon, or kosher salt. Wet the rim of the glass with a slice of orange, lemon, or lime or just a little water (use a lightly dampened paper towel), then dip the rim evenly in the garnish. Lift and tap lightly to remove the excess before turning the glass over.

VARIATIONS

SUGAR RIM	SWEET & SPICY SUGAR RIM	CINNAMON RIM
Use superfine colored sugar.	Mix equal parts sugar and chili powder.	Use cinnamon sugar.

1

*

'TIS THE SEASON COCKTAILS

Mix, shake, garnish, repeat! Here's a collection of celebratory cocktails that will add a special touch to any seasonal gathering.

Friends are always intrigued and excited when you offer an unusual drink, and what better time to offer one than during the holidays? Your guests will enjoy these playful libations adorned with fun, festive ingredients, like the bubbly Apple Pie with sparkling apple cider (page 53) or the Naughty & Nice Margarita featuring a Sweet & Spicy Sugar Rim (page 47). So grab your cocktail shaker and your favorite glass, and let's get started.

CRANBERRY SHRUB COCKTAIL

Cranberry Shrub (page 24)

3½ oz [100 ml] vodka

Ginger ale, for topping off

3 fresh cranberries, skewered, for garnish

This drink takes a couple of extra steps due to the tantalizingly tart shrub (a mixture of sugar, apple cider, and fruit), but the effort is all worth it for this delicious, healthy-ish cocktail.

Fill a highball glass halfway with crushed ice. Pour in 2 oz [60 ml] of the cranberry shrub, add the vodka, and stir. Top off with ginger ale and garnish with the cranberry skewer.

MOSCOW REINDEER

MAKES 1 DRINK

2 oz [60 ml] vodka

½ oz [15 ml] fresh lime juice (about ½ lime)

4 oz [120 ml] ginger beer

Candied ginger, for garnish

Lime wedge, for garnish

Get in the swing of the season with this gingery classic. Complete the look by serving it in a traditional copper mug—it really does make a difference!

Fill a copper mug with crushed ice. Pour in the vodka and lime juice. Top with the ginger beer, adding more to taste as needed. Garnish with a skewer of candied ginger and a lime wedge.

BERRY SMASH

MAKES 1 DRINK

½ cup [70 g] fresh or frozen and thawed berries
(such as blackberries, blueberries, or raspberries)

2 or 3 mint leaves, plus more for garnish

3 oz [90 ml] vodka

1 oz [30 ml] Simple Syrup (page 23)

Club soda, for topping off

A delightfully refreshing way to recover after a big holiday meal, this adaptable recipe can be used with a variety of berries.

Fill a tumbler with ice. Put the berries in a shaker glass. Smash the berries with a muddler or wooden spoon until they have released all their juices. Crumple the mint leaves and add to the shaker along with the vodka, simple syrup, and ice. Shake vigorously. Strain into the tumbler, leaving about 2 in [5 cm] of space at the top (you will have extra of the mixture). Top off with club soda.

WHITE CHRISTMAS

MAKES 1 DRINK

1 oz [30 ml] vodka

1 oz [30 ml] amaretto

1 oz [30 ml] heavy whipping cream

Freshly grated nutmeg, for garnish

This creamy drink could pass for melted ice cream if it weren't for the little kick at the end.

Chill a martini glass. Pour the vodka, amaretto, and heavy whipping cream into an ice-filled shaker. Shake until cold, then strain into the chilled glass. Grate a little touch of nutmeg on top.

CANDY CANE MARTINI

MAKES 1 DRINK

1½ oz [45 ml] vodka

1 oz [30 ml] club soda

1 tsp peppermint schnapps

Mini candy cane, for garnish

Here's a martini that goes down like candy. The mini candy cane adds the perfect holiday touch.

Chill a martini glass. Pour the vodka, club soda, and peppermint schnapps into an ice-filled shaker. Shake until cold, then pour into the chilled glass. Hang a mini candy cane over the rim of the glass.

BONNE FÊTE FIZZ

MAKES 1 DRINK

1 Tbsp confectioners' sugar or Simple Syrup
(page 23)

2 oz [60 ml] gin

1 oz [30 ml] fresh lemon juice

Soda water, for topping off

One 2 in [5 cm] piece cucumber,
peeled and sliced diagonally, for garnish

1 lemon round, for garnish

*This is an effervescent,
nose-tickling drink that's
perfect for the holidays.*

Fill a highball glass with ice. Pour in the sugar, gin, and lemon juice. Top off with soda water. Stir vigorously. Garnish with the cucumber and lemon.

FIGGY PUDDING

1 Tbsp fig jam

1 sugar cube

3 oz [90 ml] gin

Ginger ale, for topping off

1 Tbsp granulated sugar

1 fig, sliced

No baking is required for this play on the Victorian dessert (but it's no less delicious!).

Fill a mason jar with ice. Add the fig jam and sugar cube to a shaker, and muddle until incorporated. Add ice and the gin. Shake vigorously. Strain into the mason jar and top off with ginger ale. Spread the granulated sugar on a small plate and dip both sides of the fig slice in it. Place the sugared fig slice on the rim of the glass.

EVERGREEN SPARKLER

2 oz [60 ml] gin

2 oz [60 ml] Rosemary Syrup (page 23)

2 oz [60 ml] fresh lemon juice

Club soda, for topping off

Rosemary sprig, for garnish

This pleasingly piney drink will be a satisfying way to spread cheer after a day of decorating or a walk in a wintery forest.

Fill a tumbler glass with ice. Pour the gin, rosemary syrup, and lemon juice into an ice-filled shaker. Shake vigorously. Strain into the glass, leaving about 1 in [2.5 cm] of space at the top. Top off with club soda and garnish with a rosemary sprig.

WINTER SUNSET

MAKES 2 DRINKS

3¼ oz [96 ml] gin

1⅛ oz [33 ml] fresh lemon juice

¾ oz [23 ml] orange liqueur

1 egg white

Cheers to the end of a festive day with this citrusy beverage, perfect for sipping while gathering discarded wrapping paper.

Chill two old fashioned or coupe glasses. Pour the gin, lemon juice, orange liqueur, and egg white into an ice-filled shaker. Shake vigorously, then strain into the chilled glasses.

SANTA'S CUP

6 oz [180 ml] Pimm's

2 oz [60 ml] fresh lemon juice

1 sugar cube, crushed

Fresh cranberries, for garnish

2 tangerine slices, for garnish

1 fresh mint sprig, for garnish

Ginger ale, for topping off

An ultra-drinkable twist on the Pimm's Cup, this cocktail is ideal for sipping after indulging in some holiday cookies or sneaking some presents under the tree.

Pour the Pimm's, lemon juice, and crushed sugar cube into an ice-filled shaker. Shake vigorously. In a tumbler, drop in the cranberries, tangerine slices, mint sprig, and ice. Strain the Pimm's mixture into the prepared tumbler until half-full and top off with ginger ale.

SILVER & GOLD

3 oz [90 ml] tequila

2 oz [60 ml] Honey Syrup (page 23)

1 oz [30 ml] fresh lemon juice

Club soda, for topping off

Lemon slice, for garnish

What's a holiday celebration without a bit of silver and gold (tequila, that is)?

Pour the tequila, honey syrup, and lemon juice into an ice-filled shaker. Shake and strain into an old fashioned glass. Top off with club soda and place a lemon slice on top.

POINSETTIA COOLER

MAKES 1 DRINK

3 oz [90 ml] tequila

2 oz [60 ml] cranberry juice cocktail

1 oz [30 ml] fresh lime juice

1 to 2 oz [30 to 60 ml] Cranberry Shrub (page 24)

1 lime

Take inspiration from seasonal poinsettias and whip up this zesty cocktail with a rich holiday hue.

VARIATION: *If you don't have cranberry shrub on hand, use equal parts Simple Syrup (page 23) and cranberry juice.*

Fill an old fashioned glass or mason jar with crushed ice. Pour the tequila, cranberry juice, and lime juice into an ice-filled shaker. Shake vigorously and strain into the glass. Add a small handful more of crushed ice on top of the drink to form a small mound and drizzle the cranberry shrub over it. Grate lime zest over the top. Serve with a straw.

NAUGHTY & NICE MARGARITA

Sweet & Spicy Sugar (page 26), for garnish

1 jalapeño, seeded and sliced

3 oz [90 ml] tequila

2 oz [60 ml] Triple Sec

1 oz [30 ml] fresh lime juice

Treat yourself to something sweet and spicy, no matter where you fall on Santa's list.

Pour the Sweet & Spicy Sugar into a shallow bowl. Run a damp towel around the rim of an old fashioned glass. Dip it in the sugar mixture, making sure to completely cover the entire rim (see page 26 for more detailed instructions). Fill with ice and set aside.

Add 3 or 4 slices of jalapeño and the tequila to a shaker and muddle (30 seconds for mild, up to a minute for super hot). Add the Triple Sec, lime juice, and ice. Shake vigorously and strain into the prepared glass.

CHRISTMAS IN JULY

MAKES 1 DRINK

4 oz [120 ml] crème de coconut

4 oz [120 ml] pineapple juice

3 oz [90 ml] rum

2 or 3 dashes Angostura bitters

Sweet & Spicy Sugar (page 26), for garnish

1 pineapple wedge, for garnish

1 maraschino cherry, for garnish

Whip this up when you're craving warm summer days. Paper umbrellas are not required but highly recommended.

Combine the crème de coconut, pineapple juice, rum, and bitters in a blender with a generous cup of ice. Blend until smooth, 1 to 2 minutes. Pour into a wineglass. Spread the Sweet & Spicy Sugar on a small plate and dip both sides of the pineapple wedge in the mixture. Garnish the glass with a skewer of the prepared pineapple wedge and a maraschino cherry.

MISTLETOE KISS

2 oz [60 ml] whiskey

1 oz [30 ml] Simple Syrup (page 23)

½ oz [15 ml] fresh lemon juice

½ oz [15 ml] fresh lime juice

1 egg white

1 or 2 drops grenadine, for garnish

A riff on the classic Whiskey Sour, this deliciously zesty drink will make you pucker up—so go stand under the mistletoe!

Put a big cube of ice in an old fashioned glass or chill a coupe glass. Pour the whiskey, simple syrup, lemon juice, lime juice, and egg white into a shaker. Shake vigorously until foamy. Strain the mixture into the prepared glass. Garnish with a drop or two of grenadine.

APPLE PIE

MAKES 1 DRINK

3 oz [90 ml] whiskey

2 oz [60 ml] Honey Syrup (page 23)

1 drop vanilla extract

Sparkling apple cider, for topping off

1 apple round, for garnish

1 cinnamon stick, for garnish (optional)

This drink is easy as pie, thanks to an aromatic blend of honey, vanilla, and sparking apple cider. Drop in a cinnamon stick for a delightful way to stir it up.

Fill a tumbler or mason jar with a handful of ice. Pour the whiskey, honey syrup, and vanilla into an ice-filled shaker. Shake vigorously and strain into the glass. Top off with sparkling apple cider and garnish with a thin round of apple and a cinnamon stick, if desired.

FIRESIDE GLOW

MAKES 1 DRINK

3 oz [90 ml] bourbon

3 oz [90 ml] Cinnamon Syrup (page 23)

2 or 3 dashes amaretto liqueur

Ideal for warming up by a roaring fire, this boozy drink has comforting notes of cinnamon and almond, thanks to an elegant coating of amaretto.

Fill an old fashioned glass with ice. Pour in the bourbon and cinnamon syrup. Stir gently to combine. In a separate old fashioned glass, add a few drops of amaretto and turn the glass to coat it in the liqueur. Pour out the excess amaretto. Strain the bourbon mixture into the amaretto glass. Add one or two cubes of ice, if desired.

QUINCE OLD FASHIONED

MAKES 1 DRINK

1 tsp quince paste

1 sugar cube

1 tsp water

3 dashes Angostura bitters

2 oz [60 ml] bourbon

Orange peel, for garnish

A seasonal twist on an old fashioned, this cocktail features quince paste, which cuts through the mouth-warming bourbon with its candied tang.

In an old fashioned glass, muddle the quince paste and sugar cube until incorporated. Add the water and bitters, stirring to mix. Add the bourbon and stir gently. Garnish with an orange peel.

IT'S A WONDERFUL LIFE

MAKES 1 DRINK

3 oz [90 ml] half-and-half

1½ oz [45 ml] Irish cream liqueur

½ oz [15 ml] crème de menthe

Ground cinnamon, for garnish

If only George Bailey could have sipped one of these smooth, creamy cocktails, he would have known right away what a wonderful life he had.

Fill an old fashioned glass halfway with ice. Pour the half-and-half, Irish cream liqueur, and crème de menthe into an ice-filled shaker. Shake until cold, then strain into the prepared glass. Dust with ground cinnamon.

FLICKERING LIGHTS

1½ oz [45 ml] brandy

½ oz [15 ml] crème de menthe

Piece of gold leaf, for garnish

Brandy devotees might recognize the sting in this drink, also known as a Stinger. With a lightly minty, boozy note, it is a perfect drink to freshen up the holidays.

Pour the brandy and crème de menthe into an ice-filled shaker. Shake until cold, then strain into a martini glass. Garnish with the gold leaf.

THE SNOWBALL

MAKES 1 DRINK

2 oz [60 ml] Advocaat

2 oz [60 ml] sparkling lemonade

1 oz [30 ml] fresh lime juice

1 lemon twist, for garnish

This is a fizzy twist on creamy Scandinavian Advocaat liqueur. If you can't find this type of liqueur, feel free to replace it with eggnog. For the ultimate snowball experience, serve with spherical ice cubes.

Chill a coupe glass. Pour the Advocaat, sparkling lemonade, and lime juice into an ice-filled shaker. Shake until very cold, then strain into the chilled glass. Garnish with a lemon twist.

2

*

FESTIVE CHAMPAGNE SIPPERS

Whether you serve it at a Christmas Day brunch or on New Year's Eve, there's no other beverage that marks a celebration like champagne.

Ah, those lovely light bubbles dancing on your tongue! The uncorking is always an event, and the sparkling effervescence of the drink makes it a true party-pleaser.

VELVET RIBBON

MAKES 1 DRINK

3 oz [90 ml] champagne

3 oz [90 ml] lambic beer

1 oz [30 ml] Chambord or raspberry liqueur

Delectably smooth and pleasing to the palette, this take on a Black Velvet gets a jammy twist with the addition of lambic, a tart and fruity Belgium-brewed beer.

Pour the champagne into a coupe or flute glass. Top with the lambic and Chambord.

SNOW DAY

1 Tbsp sugar

3 fresh or frozen and thawed blueberries,
for garnish

4 oz [120 ml] champagne

2 oz [60 ml] elderflower liqueur,
such as St-Germain

*Fragrant elderflower
liqueur gives champagne
an extra boost of
sophistication in this
simple yet elegant drink.*

Spread the sugar on a small plate, wet the blueberries with water, and then roll them in the sugar; place on a skewer. Freeze until ready to use.

Pour the champagne and elderflower liqueur into a champagne flute or coupe glass. Garnish with the blueberry skewer.

SANTA BABY

½ oz [15 ml] Chambord

5 oz [150 ml] champagne

5 or 6 pomegranate seeds

Ring in the New Year with this delightful crimson cocktail. Every time you take a sip, pomegranate seeds will rise and fall, dancing in the champagne bubbles.

Pour the Chambord into a champagne flute or other tall glass, then add the champagne. Finish by dropping the seeds into the cocktail.

HOLIDAY BELLINI

MAKES 1 DRINK

1 oz [30 ml] apricot nectar, chilled

4 oz [120 ml] champagne, chilled

3 fresh cranberries, for garnish

Here's a winter version of the famous classic that originated at Harry's Bar in Venice. This recipe uses apricot nectar to give the drink a warm glow.

Pour the apricot nectar into a coupe glass. Fill to the top with champagne and stir. Place the cranberries on a skewer and rest it on the rim of the glass.

RUDOLPH'S RED-NOSED COCKTAIL

MAKES 1 DRINK

1 sugar cube

Drop of Angostura bitters

4 oz [120 ml] champagne

Splash of Campari

A splash of Campari makes this sweet and bubbly libation shine bright (you might even say it glows).

Place the sugar cube in a champagne flute or other footed glass. Add a drop of the Angostura bitters to the sugar cube. Add the champagne and Campari.

PARTRIDGE IN A PEAR TREE

MAKES 1 DRINK

1 oz [30 ml] pear eau de vie

4 to 5 oz [120 to 150 ml] champagne

1 frozen pear wedge or strip of pear,
for garnish

This fresh, wintry cocktail works only if both the pear liqueur and the champagne are well chilled. If you like, rim the glass with citrus juice and dip in sugar.

Pour the pear eau de vie into a champagne flute or a coupe glass. Fill the rest of the glass with champagne. Garnish with a frozen pear wedge.

FRENCH KISS

1 oz [30 ml] Lillet

4 oz [120 ml] champagne

1 orange twist, for garnish

This cocktail uses Lillet, a French aperitif made from herbs, wine, and brandy. Its distinctive flavor adds sophistication to this delicate cocktail.

Pour the Lillet into a champagne flute or a coupe glass. Add the champagne and stir. Twist the orange peel over the drink and drop it in.

SNOWY MORNING MIMOSA

MAKES 1 DRINK

2 oz [60 ml] white cranberry juice

4 oz [120 ml] champagne

1 or 2 fresh cranberries, for garnish (optional)

This light version of the classic brunch drink is the perfect pairing with a breakfast spread or washed down with some sweet holiday cookies.

VARIATION: *Create mimosas for a crowd by multiplying the recipe by the number of guests and pouring the juice and champagne mixture into a pitcher.*

Pour the cranberry juice and champagne into an ice-filled shaker. Shake until cold, then strain into a flute. Add the cranberries for garnish, if desired.

KIR ROYALE

MAKES 1 DRINK

Superfine sugar, for garnish

½ oz [15 ml] crème de cassis

½ tsp fresh lime juice (optional)

5 oz [150 ml] champagne

This lovely aperitif gets its pale cranberry hue from crème de cassis, a black currant–flavored liqueur with a light berry flavor. You can add a little lime juice to temper the sweetness, if you like.

Pour the superfine sugar into a shallow bowl. Run a damp towel around the rim of a champagne flute and dip the rim into the sugar bowl, making sure to cover the entire rim in sugar. Tap off the excess. Pour the crème de cassis and lime juice (if using) into the sugared champagne flute. Add the champagne. Stir.

3

✳

WARM & TOASTY TODDIES

What could be more comforting when you come in from the cold than placing your hands around a glass filled with a steaming-hot, flavorful drink?

As you take your first sip, the chill slips away and you feel relaxed and warm all over. Because hot toddies are made individually and not served from a communal bowl, it's a little tricky to serve them to a large crowd without letting them get cold. You might consider putting all the ingredients on the table and allowing your guests to mix their toddies, minus the hot liquid, which you can pour yourself to avoid accidents.

NUTCRACKER SWEET

MAKES 1 DRINK

½ oz [15 ml] crème de cacao

½ oz [15 ml] amaretto

6 to 8 oz [180 to 240 ml] hot coffee

2 Tbsp coffee ice cream

Sliced almonds, for garnish

Just like its namesake, this comforting drink will make you think of the holidays. Grab a couple of shortbread cookies and sip it by the fire.

Pour the crème de cacao and amaretto into an Irish coffee glass. Add coffee, leaving 1 in [2.5 cm] of space at the top. Stir until blended. Top with coffee ice cream and sliced almonds.

HOT MINT CHOCOLATE

MAKES 1 DRINK

1 oz [30 ml] peppermint schnapps

8 oz [240 ml] hot chocolate

Marshmallows, for garnish

Peppermint stick, for garnish (optional)

This crowd-pleaser can be made as plain hot chocolate for the kids or with a little kick for the adults. Stir with a peppermint stick for best results.

VARIATION: *For the kid-friendly version, add 1 or 2 drops of mint extract to the hot chocolate instead of the schnapps, and sandwich a toasted marshmallow between two Peppermint Patties on a skewer.*

Pour the peppermint schnapps into a glass mug. Fill to the top with hot chocolate. Place the marshmallows on a metal skewer and toast over a stove burner on low heat until medium brown, or to your desired char. Float the toasted marshmallows on top of the drink or slip them onto a cocktail skewer and rest it across the glass. Garnish with a peppermint stick, if desired.

HOT BUTTERED APPLE CIDER

MAKES 1 DRINK

8 oz [240 ml] apple cider

1½ oz [45 ml] butterscotch schnapps

Whipped Cream, unsweetened (page 25), for topping

1 apple slice, for garnish

This yummy drink tastes like a melted toffee bar. Try this buttery, rich sipper with a crisp almond biscotti.

Pour the apple cider into a medium saucepan and warm over medium heat until simmering. Pour the warm apple cider into an Irish coffee glass or an old fashioned glass. Add the butterscotch schnapps, then top with whipped cream. Garnish with the apple slice.

THE BLITZEN

1 oz [30 ml] Irish cream liqueur

1 oz [30 ml] dark rum

½ oz [15 ml] crème de cacao

8 oz [240 ml] hot chocolate

Whipped Cream (page 25), for topping

Cocoa powder, for garnish

Perfect for sipping after sledding, this decadently creamy drink will warm you up on the coldest of nights.

Pour the Irish cream liqueur, dark rum, and crème de cacao into an Irish coffee glass. Add hot chocolate, leaving 1 in [2.5 cm] of space at the top. Top with whipped cream and add a dash of cocoa powder.

HOT BUTTERED RUM

MAKES 1 DRINK

1 tsp brown sugar

4 to 6 oz [120 to 180 ml] boiling water

1½ oz [45 ml] dark rum

1 Tbsp butter

Freshly grated nutmeg, for garnish

Lore has it that in the eighteenth century, American politicians used this warm concoction to woo supporters. The butter adds a silky texture to this delightful classic.

Put the brown sugar into a heatproof glass punch cup and fill two-thirds full with boiling water. Add the rum and butter. Wait until the butter melts, then stir and sprinkle a little nutmeg on top.

HOT BUTTERED WINE

MAKES 1 DRINK

6 oz [180 ml] dessert wine,
such as sherry or port

2½ oz [75 ml] water

2 tsp maple syrup

1 tsp butter

Freshly grated nutmeg, for garnish

This is a good alternative to the more potent Hot Buttered Rum (facing page). The mingled scents of maple syrup and wine will soothe your nerves while the heat warms you.

Add the wine and water to a medium saucepan and warm over medium heat to just simmering; do not allow to boil. Pour the heated wine mixture into a glass and add the maple syrup and butter. Stir and sprinkle with a little nutmeg.

IRISH COFFEE

MAKES 1 DRINK

2 tsp raw sugar, preferably demerara

1½ oz [45 ml] Irish whiskey

6 to 8 oz [180 to 240 ml] hot coffee

Whipped Cream (page 25), for topping

You don't want to mess with this classic. It's best when prepared in the most traditional fashion, using demerara sugar.

Put the sugar in an Irish coffee glass. Add the Irish whiskey and coffee, leaving 1 in [2.5 cm] of space at the top. Top with whipped cream.

HOT BRANDY ALEXANDER

MAKES 1 DRINK

4 oz [120 ml] whole milk

¾ oz [23 ml] brandy

¾ oz [23 ml] crème de cacao

Whipped Cream (page 25), for topping

Chocolate shavings, for garnish

Brandy is a delightful after-dinner drink, but if you're looking for something a little sweeter and a little richer, this is the drink for you. Dip biscotti into that pillowy whipped cream . . . this must be heaven.

Heat the milk in a small saucepan over medium heat until very warm. Pour the brandy and crème de cacao into a mug, then add the heated milk. Stir until blended. Top with whipped cream and chocolate shavings.

4

*

HOLIDAY
PARTY
PUNCHES

Punches are an easy way to serve a drink to a large crowd— perfect for holiday get-togethers.

The very sight of a punch bowl says "party," and the smells, colors, and flavors of these seasonal brews make any occasion festive. Their unpretentious charm also makes them good candidates for an afternoon open house or a casual potluck.

NEW YEAR'S DAY BLOODY MARY BAR

MAKES 8 DRINKS

32 oz [960 ml] Clamato

8 oz [240 ml] vodka

4 tsp creamed horseradish

1 tsp Worcestershire sauce

1 tsp Tabasco

Salt and freshly ground black pepper

GARNISH BAR

Celery stalks

Stuffed olives

Pepperoncini

Marinated pearl onions

Kosher pickle spears

Diced pepper Jack cheese

2 lemons, quartered

continued

Up your brunch game with this impressive spread. The list of suggested garnishes is just a starting point—anything salty, briny, or savory can make a fun addition (Bacon! Pickled carrots! Dill sprigs!)—the sky's the limit.

Combine the Clamato, vodka, horseradish, Worcestershire sauce, and Tabasco in a large glass pitcher. Add salt and pepper to taste. Stir vigorously. Arrange the garnish bar toppings in separate tumbler and old fashioned glasses, with smaller items (such as olives, pepperoncini, pearl onions, diced cheese) pre-skewered.

Serve in tall highball glasses filled with ice. Squeeze a lemon quarter over each drink and drop into the glass before adding the desired garnishes.

'TIS THE SEASON SANGRIA

MAKES 8 DRINKS

¼ cup [50 g] sugar

8 oz [240 ml] water

2 oz [60 ml] fresh orange juice

1 oz [30 ml] fresh lemon juice

1 cinnamon stick

24 oz [720 ml] red wine

6 oz [180 ml] sparkling water

1 oz [30 ml] Cointreau

4 oranges, thinly sliced, for garnish

½ lemon, thinly sliced, for garnish

½ lime, thinly sliced, for garnish

½ Pippin or Granny Smith apple,
cored and thinly sliced, for garnish

20 grapes, green and red, for garnish

continued

This version of the classic fruity punch is made with Cointreau, which adds a distinctive orange flavor. It's best served cold (but not with ice, because it would dilute the flavor); try freezing some extra sangria in an ice cube tray to add when serving.

Place the sugar, water, orange and lemon juices, and cinnamon stick in a saucepan and bring to a boil over medium-high heat. Lower the heat and simmer for 10 minutes. Remove from the heat and let cool. Pour the red wine, sparkling water, and Cointreau into a punch bowl. Remove the cinnamon stick from the syrup, then pour the syrup into the punch bowl. Float the fruit on top. Chill for at least an hour before serving.

GLÖGG

MAKES 10 TO 12 DRINKS

32 oz [960 ml] red wine

32 oz [960 ml] aquavit

Peel of 1 orange

4 cloves

2 cardamom pods

8 sugar cubes

Blanched whole almonds, for garnish

Raisins, for garnish

This spicy Scandinavian brew is sure to bring holiday cheer.

Place the red wine and aquavit in separate saucepans and warm each over medium heat. Place the orange peel, cloves, and cardamom pods in the red wine, bring to a simmer, and cook for 10 minutes. Strain. Place the sugar cubes in a heated punch bowl, then add the strained heated wine and the aquavit. To serve, heat mugs. Place several almonds and raisins in each mug, then fill with the glögg and serve.

BLUE CHRISTMAS PUNCH

MAKES 8 DRINKS

16 oz [480 ml] blueberry juice

16 oz [480 ml] pomegranate juice

4 oz [120 ml] fresh lemon juice

12 oz [360 ml] gin

3 oz [90 ml] Simple Syrup (page 23)

Blueberry-Lemon-Rosemary Ice Ring (page 25)

Sparkling lemon water, for topping off

This fruit-forward mixture will impress guests thanks to an effortless ice ring. If you don't have access to a Bundt pan, make it mini by freezing each ingredient in individual ice cube trays.

Pour the blueberry juice, pomegranate juice, lemon juice, gin, and simple syrup into a large punch bowl. Stir to combine. When ready to serve, add the prepared ice ring (run a bit of warm water over the outside of the pan to loosen). To serve, ladle into punch cups. Top off each cup with a splash of sparkling lemon water.

FEZZIWIG PUNCH

MAKES 8 TO 10 DRINKS

Lemon slices, cut into quarters,
plus more for garnish

24 oz [720 ml] black tea

24 oz [720 ml] lemonade

6 oz [180 ml] dark rum

6 oz [180 ml] Grand Marnier

4 oz [120 ml] Honey Syrup (page 23)

No one can resist this incredibly palatable punch, which is sure to please even the grumpiest of scrooges.

Place a quarter slice of lemon into each compartment of an ice cube tray and fill with water. Freeze until solid, 2 to 3 hours. Save until ready to serve the punch.

Pour the remaining ingredients into a large punch bowl and stir. Add the lemon slice ice. Garnish each serving with extra lemon slices.

CLASSIC EGGNOG

12 eggs, separated

¾ cup [150 g] plus 3 Tbsp superfine sugar

24 oz [720 ml] whole milk

16 oz [480 ml] heavy whipping cream

12 oz [360 ml] dark rum

Freshly grated nutmeg, for garnish

This eggnog is creamy but not too rich, sweet but not cloying, and full-bodied without being too thick. Using real eggs, rather than an eggnog mix, makes an enormous difference in taste and texture.

ALCOHOL-FREE VARIATION:
Make without the rum, adding another 8 oz [240 ml] milk.

In a large mixing bowl, beat the egg yolks well. Add ¾ cup [150 g] of the sugar and mix until thick. Stir in the milk, 8 oz [240 ml] of the cream, and the rum. Cover and chill. Beat the egg whites in a large mixing bowl until frothy, gradually adding the remaining 3 Tbsp of sugar, beating until soft peaks form. Fold the egg whites and remaining 8 oz [240 ml] of cream into the cold yolk mixture. Ladle into punch cups and sprinkle with nutmeg.

JOLLY FRUITY CIDER

MAKES 12 DRINKS

32 oz [960 ml] apple cider

12 oz [360 ml] club soda

4 oz [120 ml] brandy

2 oz [60 ml] orange liqueur

8 tsp confectioners' sugar or Simple Syrup (page 23)

½ orange, thinly sliced into rounds

½ crisp red apple, quartered, cored, and thinly sliced

½ Bosc pear, quartered, cored, and thinly sliced

12 mint sprigs, for garnish

Use high-quality apple cider for the best flavor. Serve this punch alongside delicate Christmas sugar cookies and candied nuts.

Fill a large punch bowl with ice. Pour in the apple cider, club soda, brandy, and orange liqueur. Add the sugar, then stir vigorously. Float the fruit on top. Serve in red wineglasses, or another glass with a wide rim, garnished with a mint sprig.

WASSAIL

MAKES 8 DRINKS

1 cinnamon stick

6 cloves

6 whole allspice berries

48 oz [1.4 L] apple cider

16 oz [480 ml] cranberry juice

¾ oz [23 ml] Simple Syrup (page 23)

4 oz [120 ml] Calvados

4 oz [120 ml] brandy

1 Pippin or Granny Smith apple,
quartered, cored, and thinly sliced, for garnish

This traditional Norwegian punch gets its name from an old toast—it literally means "be in good health."

Wrap the spices in cheesecloth and tie with string. Place the apple cider, cranberry juice, simple syrup, and spices in a stockpot, bring to a simmer over medium heat, and cook for 8 to 10 minutes. Add the Calvados and brandy, and cook for 1 to 2 minutes. Remove the sachet. Serve in heatproof cups, topped with an apple slice.

5

*

ZERO-PROOF LIBATIONS

When planning a party, there's no reason to feel that drinks without alcohol are without distinction.

Each of these nonalcoholic drinks has its own unique flavor and flair and is equally festive in appearance. You'll find a variety of choices, from cold drinks to hot mocktails to communal punches. For an alcohol-free variation of Classic Eggnog, see page 106.

GRAPEFRUIT SHRUB MOCKTAIL

Grapefruit Shrub (page 25)

1 oz [30 ml] Simple Syrup (page 23), plus more as needed

Club soda, for topping off

A restorative option after having one too many holiday treats, this shrub is also wonderful poured over gelato or added to lemonade.

Fill a tumbler glass with ice. Pour 2 oz [60 ml] of the shrub into the tumbler, add the simple syrup, and top off with club soda. Stir, adding more simple syrup to taste.

GINGERSNAP PUNCH

MAKES 8 DRINKS

48 oz [1.4 L] ginger ale

3 oz [90 ml] fresh lime juice

2 oz [60 ml] Raspberry Syrup (page 24)

8 candied lime slices (page 24), for garnish

This punch is popular with both kids and adults. Be sure to use fresh lime juice, or it won't have the necessary zip.

Fill a large glass punch bowl with ice. Pour in the ginger ale, lime juice, and raspberry syrup. Stir. Serve in glass punch cups, garnished with a slice of candied lime.

CRANBERRY SAUCE MOCKTAIL

MAKES 1 DRINK

6 oz [180 ml] cranberry juice cocktail

2 oz [60 ml] club soda

½ oz [15 ml] fresh lime juice

1 tsp fresh orange juice

1 lime twist, for garnish

This drink has many of the same ingredients as the seasonal relish we expect to see during the holidays.

Fill a red wineglass with crushed ice. Pour the cranberry juice into the wineglass, add the club soda, lime juice, and orange juice, then stir. Garnish with a lime twist.

WINTERTIME TEA

4 oz [120 ml] lemonade

4 oz [120 ml] black tea,
cooled to room temperature

2 oz [60 ml] Rosemary Syrup (page 23),
plus more as needed

Lemon wheel, for garnish

The light and refreshing summertime drink gets a seasonal twist with a piney note of rosemary. For a punch of fizz, use a sparkling lemonade.

Fill a tumbler glass with ice. Pour the lemonade, black tea, and rosemary syrup into the tumbler. Stir, adding more syrup to taste. Garnish with a lemon wheel.

HOT VANILLA CREAM

MAKES 1 DRINK

8 oz [240 ml] whole milk

3 Tbsp malted milk powder

1½ tsp vanilla extract

Whipped Cream (page 25), for topping

Freshly grated nutmeg, for garnish

Ground cinnamon, for garnish

Looking for something cozy, like a pair of soft, fuzzy cashmere socks? If so, you'll enjoy this exceedingly subtle, gentle drink, perfect for dipping Christmas cookies.

Heat the milk in a small saucepan over medium heat until very hot. Add the malted milk powder and vanilla, and whisk until slightly foamy. Pour into a mug and top with several dollops of whipped cream. Sprinkle with a little nutmeg and cinnamon, if desired.

MULLED CIDER

64 oz [2 L] apple cider

1 oz [30 ml] maple syrup

1 lemon, thinly sliced into rounds,
plus 1 lemon peel

1 orange, thinly sliced into rounds,
plus 1 orange peel

2 tsp ground nutmeg

2 tsp ground cinnamon

2 cinnamon sticks

Warm, fragrant, and delicious . . . a winter classic.

Pour the cider and maple syrup into a large saucepan and bring to a simmer over medium heat. Add the remaining ingredients and stir to combine. Simmer for 15 minutes. To serve, ladle into heatproof punch cups.

FOAMY MEXICAN HOT CHOCOLATE

MAKES 1 DRINK

8 oz [240 ml] whole milk

2 wedges Mexican hot chocolate

Marshmallows, for garnish (optional)

Whipped Cream (page 25), for garnish (optional)

Mexican hot chocolate usually comes in a round box with four ¾ in [2 cm] disks of 8 wedges. The chocolate can be found in some supermarkets, specialty food stores, and Latin American groceries. It has a more complex taste and fragrance than your average hot chocolate, with hints of cinnamon, almonds, and vanilla.

Heat the milk in a small saucepan over medium heat until very hot. In a blender, pulse the chocolate wedges until coarsely chopped. Add the hot milk and blend until smooth. Serve in a mug, adding marshmallows or fresh whipped cream, if desired.

TABLE OF EQUIVALENTS

VOLUME EQUIVALENTS

AMERICAN	METRIC	FLUID OZ
¼ tsp	1.25 ml	
½ tsp	2.5 ml	
1 tsp	5 ml	
1½ tsp (½ Tbsp)	7.5 ml	
1 Tbsp (3 tsp)	15 ml	
2 Tbsp	30 ml	1 fl oz
3 Tbsp	45 ml	1½ fl oz
¼ cup (4 Tbsp)	60 ml	2 fl oz
⅓ cup (5 Tbsp)	80 ml	2½ fl oz
½ cup (8 Tbsp)	120 ml	4 fl oz
¾ cup (12 Tbsp)	180 ml	6 fl oz
1 cup (16 Tbsp)	240 ml	8 fl oz
4½ cups	1 L	
6½ cups	1.5 L	
8 cups (2 qt)	2 L	

LENGTH EQUIVALENTS

INCHES	MM/CM
¼	6 mm
½	12 mm
¾	2 cm
1	2.5 cm
1½	4 cm
2	5 cm

INDEX